Preface:

He slams his hand on my PC, which quickly opens a screen filled with thousands of call contacts, 'pick up the phone and start making us money", he said!

I was terrified, confused, and trembling, and thought my boss was a complete jerk! How can anyone make money with just a telephone, and a random list of businesses.

The thought of picking up the phone and talking to a complete stranger who was likely going to tell me to go away seemed a bit scary. It seemed like a great time to become a chain smoker, just so I could avoid picking up the phone and hearing that dreaded 'I'm not Interested'.

6 months later I was making more money, then I could count! After my first month the pay cheque arrived, a whopping 7,000 pounds, this is awesome I thought 'I can really make this much money' I felt like a Rock Star. I shouted drinks every Friday and bought expensive toys, I honestly felt invincible.

And then, one day I saw a customer service rep crying in the lunch room, the reason shocked me; I had no idea that customers were rarely getting past their first project. I heard a bunch of rumours that the company was terrible and run poorly I even called an ex-client by accident and they started yelling at me.

My first sales job was a real opener to the reality of working for a company, the good, the bad, and the ugly!

Fast forward 13 years and who would have thought that this first job would lead me to run a successful 'Telemarketing Agency' in Asia; a task I had originally hated had now become my passion, and life, this was to become something I lived and breathed every day.

Here is what I learned!

Index:

1. I made 250,000 Calls., this is what I learned!

Spending over 12 years in sales across multiple industries has certainly offered its fair share of wins and losses throughout my career.

Just the other day I calculated that over my working life I have been employed in over 11 sales positions, executed around 150 sales campaigns, and made over 250,000 cold calls.

Through trial and error, I managed to gather enough knowledge, tips, tricks, and experience to create a proven system. This 'system' can be engineered into pretty much any B2B phone campaign which delivers success, meets strict expectations and achieves quality results.

Below I have outlined the six crucial ingredients when looking to run a successful B2B Lead Generation program which you can use as a guideline when planning your next campaign.

5.1   Can I Sell it?

The first question you have to ask yourself before running a B2B lead generation campaign for your business or your company is 'Can I Sell It?'

If you cannot honestly believe in what you are selling, and do not show some sort of passion for the solution, product or service, how can you possibly expect someone else to buy into the idea, or provide the right training for the sales rep who will be executing the campaign?

This kind of goes for anything in life; if you are passionate about something, a hobby, a new business, (even your spouse!) you will thrive naturally to the next steps of greatness.

My advice here is to make sure as a business owner, or Sales Director that you invest time in re-igniting the fire that once gave you the passion you had to sell your product or solution.

Whether it be IT Managed Services, Cloud Software, Financial Products, Real Estate... or a unique offering to the market, it is critical that you get involved with others within the same industry, watch product demos, speak to existing clients who have gained positive results from your offerings, or even just socialize with others and reignite that passion.

Top Tip:

Back when I was running my own team with a large IT Vendor in Sydney, I made many mistakes, and one of the most critical things I learned to drive the right results were getting the right energy, motivation, and attitude from the sales team, plus getting them to buy into the idea which gave the team the success we were looking for.

Once you know you have the passion, and knowledge to get others excited about your services, it is time to ask yourself a very critical question. "Who is My Target Market?" Or "Which Industries Would Benefit the Most from My Offerings?"

This will truly help you to be very targeted and strategic when running new B2B Sales Campaigns. Not only will you understand who your true buyers are, but you can also even test the water and pitch your solution to a new industry and obtain real-time intelligence on how they respond to the offering. All without potentially spending thousands of dollars on marketing brochures, website and social media overhauling!

Spend some time looking at the market, and what others within your space are doing. Research by visiting similar websites to your own, reading case studies completed within your sector and relate this to the industry you need to target.

The chances are if others have had at least some success targeting a similar offering to that industry then it may be worth investigating further.

Top Tip:

During the early days of my business, I always assumed that the client outsourcing their led gen would know the most appropriate target market, and it took me several prospect calls to identify that another target market might be better suited for the client's offerings.

5.3   What About the Data?

Right, so you now have an offering that gets you out of bed in the morning, that you are truly passionate about, plus you have at least a few ideas to which industries to start targeting.

So, you are looking to create a B2B lead generation strategy.... resources are ready to go. But wait, who do I call? Where is the data?

From personal experience within my current Lead Prospecting Business, and from many years of executing sales initiatives for others, I can tell you that if you use poor data, or are expecting your sales rep(s) to create their own lists from using the web or a generic directory (breaking rule #2)... then the B2B tele-prospecting campaign will end with poor results.

It is critical that your campaign has not only the right type of data that contains the prospects name, phone number, and job titles that you need to target, but you also need to make sure you have enough data to run through the duration of the campaign.

For example, if you are estimating that you, your employee, or outsourced provider is going to make 40-50 calls a day over a 1 month (20-day campaign) then you would need at least 1,000 records (or targets) to make sure your campaign is fuelled throughout the entire period.

Top Tip:

During my sales career, I wish I had spent more time with Marketing, and line managers truly identifying the target market so it suited what I was selling, and having at least 1-2 backup targets to experiment with, and enough data for each.

5.4   Creating a Pitch that Drives the Conversation Flow.

You may have the passion, the target market, and now the data all ticked off the list, but have you thought about the sales pitch, and call structure that will be executed during the calling? It is critical that you make every call count, so knowing how to open a conversation with the right decision maker will help you to qualify for genuine interest.

During my sales career, I have used several scripts, attended dozens of sales training sessions from top quality vendors, tried and tested a whole range of cold calling approaches to get the prospect talking.

The key I have found is making sure you have a pitch that is:

·   To the point (gets the concept across)

·   Covers your existing client work, and their ROI

·   Will get your prospect talking.

…Followed by a set of qualification questions that is going to help you gain as much intelligence from the prospect as possible to guide the call to a close and get that next step required.

Remember you don't want to vomit on your target! The trick is to consult your prospect, find out about their business, what are their plans? What are their pains? Are they aligned in a way you might be able to help them reach their goal or fix their pain?

Truly understand your potential client, and they will trust you. At the very least it will help you have the best chance to qualify a genuine prospect.

Top Tip:

It took me a few years to identify and create a universal approach that could be applied to almost anything you are selling. Creating a script is great, but use them as a guideline only, and remember to talk to your prospects like normal human beings, be friendly, ask questions, and be consultative.

During my early career as a telesales rep for a medium sized telemarketing company, the thought of picking up the phone and talking to a stranger who was likely going to tell me to go away seemed a bit scary. It seemed like a great time to become a chain smoker, just so I could avoid picking up the phone and hearing that dreaded 'I'm not Interested'.

Sales have taught me many things over the years; however, on top of my list is one element that is sometimes missed when running B2B Lead Generation Campaigns, Discipline!!

If you, your sales rep(s), or your outsourced provider does not lock in time during the day to pick up the phones and make the dials, with minimal distractions then you may not get the results you are looking for.

There are plenty of distractions in the office: mobile phones, social media, smoke breaks, colleagues, etc. however you need to make sure that as an employee or business owner you are disciplined, and mature enough to lock yourself away and have the confidence to numb out distractions.

Top Tip:

One of the hardest comments I had ever heard in my sales career was hearing from my manager that I needed discipline, and structure when it came to my daily cold calling schedule.

I admit, at first, I took this to heart, however, once I started disciplining myself and locking down time to make calls throughout the day, I started seeing the fruits of all my hard work come to life.

We all know that sales are a numbers game, the more doors we knock, or people we call the chances are someone is eventually going to budge. But what about the NO's? we sometimes forget that collecting the NO's can be as valuable, if not more than the yeses.

During your sales campaigns, collecting the NO's from every call will not only provide your business with real-time intelligence on what your market is saying about your offerings but also provide the opportunity for you to develop your solutions so they meet the needs of your target market.

Think about this for a moment; how much would you spend on a new marketing brochure? commercial? website? or even a new feature or benefit of your solution? How sure are you that you your products or services meet your target markets expectations?

Top Tips:

Having a long-term lead generation strategy will help set your business up for success and provide you with the right knowledge to make sure you are sailing your business in the right direction.

2. Pick Up the Phone and Start Dialling

Working in sales for over 12 years across multiple industries, pitching multiple solutions, making dial after dial, after dial, has certainly helped to improve my confidence over the phone, accept rejection, and ultimately get more sales.

But it has not been easy!!

Just the other day I calculated that over my working life I have been employed in over 11 sales positions, executed around 150 sales campaigns, and made thousands upon thousands of cold calls.

Every sales rep, field rep, inside sales, and tele-prospector knows that cold calling can be very rewarding, and at the same time very draining. Call after call, rejection after rejection, just how do you stay motivated?

Through years of calling, trial and error, I have over time created several strategies to help stay motivated while cold calling, to help keep the energy levels flying high as much as possible throughout the working day.

Below I have outlined a few crucial tips for you to stay motivated, increase the number of calls you make, and at the same time get the most out of every cold call.

5.1   Hit the Phones - Be Disciplined.

Yes, you need to be disciplined; and yes it may sound obvious, however, it is certainly an area that most salespeople can improve on.

During my early career as a telesales rep for a medium sized telemarketing company, the thought of picking up the phone and talking to a stranger who was likely going to tell me to go away seemed a bit scary. It seemed like a great time to become a chain smoker, just so I could avoid picking up the phone and hearing that dreaded 'I'm not Interested'.

If you, your sales rep(s), or your outsourced provider does not lock in time during the day to pick up the phones and make the dials, with minimal distractions then you may not get the results you are looking for.

So, your typical workday; you come into the office, you sit at your desk, you say to yourself, yes 9:30 am I will start dialing. 9:30 am comes along, you get your 3rd email from your manager asking you for yet another excel report, 10:30 am comes along 'it's break time'. Okay so it's 11 are you start to make a few calls, but wait your colleague asks for help on a critical project; before you know it is lunch time, then you have that 2 pm meeting (where did all the time go)?

There are plenty of distractions in the office: mobile phones, social media, smoke breaks, colleagues, etc. however you need to make sure that as an employee or business owner you are disciplined, and mature enough to lock yourself away and have the confidence to numb out distractions.

Top Tips:

One of the hardest criticisms I had ever received in my sales career was hearing from my manager that I needed discipline, and structure when it came to my daily cold calling schedule.

I admit, at first, I took this to heart, however, once I started disciplining myself and locking down time to make calls throughout the day, I started seeing the fruits of all my hard work come to life.

Close your Inbox, turn off notifications, close skype messenger – Yes, your colleagues can wait.

Put up a sign and set limits – 'I am cold calling, no distractions unless the building is burning down' – Seems silly? But is it? – Set a trend, and make sure colleagues respect the fact that you are busy.

Limit breaks – Are you a smoker? – Stop chain smoking just so you don't have to cold call – a) it is bad for you and b) you will lose valuable time away from the phone – Set break times, and stick to them as much as possible.

Give yourself breathing space – Take breaks – (Yes totally contradicting my previous point, however, you need to take short-term strict (timed) breaks throughout the day, to recharge your batteries.

Exercise – Cold calling can be very draining, go for a lunchtime stroll, after work jog, hit the gym, you will feel more energized the next day.

Make it Fun – But how? – have fun on the phones; you are talking to normal human beings, crack a joke (professional of course) – "Hear it's raining cats and dogs again, - (Check the online weather) – another day in paradise" – "Thank god it's Friday' – How are you? 'Pushing through the day, were nearly there' – Be human, and you will receive human responses – (Maybe you will forget you are cold calling, and just having a normal conversation) – How cool is that!

Shine with Confidence – Pretend you are a CEO; be strong (but professional and polite) with your tone, you will get put through – Don't sound like every other sales guy out there. If Richard Branson or Bill Gates called up one of your prospect companies and asked for a C-Level executive, do you think he would be put through?

5.7   <u>Objection Handling</u> - Explore the No's

We all know that sales are a numbers game, in my previous article I mentioned how important it is to get the most out of every call; Especially the NO's? we sometimes forget that collecting the NO's can be as valuable, if not more than the yeses.

How often do you make a call, hear 'I'm just not interested, we already have that solution, we use that already, we don't have the budget for that, and blah blah blah, the list goes on and on; objection after objection.

Have you thought to ask why? That's it just one simple word why? Why are you not interested; why do you think it is too expensive, how can you possibly say there is no budget when you don't know the true value of the solutions, or product?

Start fighting the objections and collect the noes from every call you make. This will not only provide your business with real-time intelligence on what your market is saying about your offerings but also provide the opportunity for you to develop your solutions so they meet the needs of your target market.

The more objections you can overcome the better your chances to get that sales meeting with a potential client, qualify an interested, and ultimately in time get the sale, improve your sales commission, and bottom end.

Lessons Learned:

Having a long-term lead generation strategy will help set your business or career up for success and provide you with the right knowledge to make sure you are sailing in the right direction.

Always ask why? – Objections are roadblocks that can be pushed out the way, or you can turn around and head in another direction. – Actually, both work very well 1) By fighting the objection you can find a workaround, however, if you feel there is no hope then 2) you can move on to the next call.

Agree that you understand the objection – Confirm that you understand your prospects issue – really understand the true meaning. And for example, if they come at you with a strong objection like 'Oh we just don't have the budget', we are trying to cut costs etc.' respond back with another question 'Oh I understand that cutting costs is important to you, actually you know what Mr. Prospect allot of my clients say the same thing; 'perhaps you could tell me why cutting costs is so important to you?

Do your research – Who are you calling? Are they the right person? Who else can I call? Is the company in the media? Does the CIO I am calling have any recent articles online? – Any inside intel on your prospect, work history, may help you establish rapport, and trust on that first call. And you never know, you could have both worked for the same company in the past, or know the same connections on linked-in.

Plan your Strategy – Are you just going to pick up the phone, call the data list and hope for the best; well that's great, sales can be a numbers game, but why not increase your chances of success. Trying to get in front of a CIO who works for a T1, and T2 company can be near enough impossible; however, if you utilize the outside contacts, EA's (who will be your best friend) they may be able to get you in front of them, or worst case refer you onto someone else who can help you.

Use the tools around you – As salespeople do we truly utilize all the tools available to us. Take linked-in for example; do you realize just how powerful this platform is. Need to build a sales list, find any CIO, CEO, IT Director on this planet with just a few simple steps. Many industries including accountancy firms, real estate agents, and health (practices) show the key business partners, and contacts directly on the website – (sometimes you can even find their cell phone number listed).

3. How One Email Changed my Life?

Impossible, it can't be done, give up, why bother,
focus your efforts locally.

Sitting in my London office back in 2008, fresh out of University, ambition and motivation were on overdrive. Staring at the top performer board and seeing my name light up with colour, gave me a great feeling of achievement. But something was missing, there seemed to be an emptiness that could not be fulfilled with my existing life and career.

But why? here I was in my first sales job, killing my sales targets, living in one of the best cities in the world, with a great social life. Perhaps it was the gloomy winter weather, looking out of my office window at 4 pm in the afternoon and seeing pitch black.

After spending over a year traveling, and backpacking around Australia, I had returned to my home country, feeling let's just say a bit sad. Why was I sad? I wanted more, I wanted to change, I wanted to break away from the herd of sheep.

So, after many weeks of pondering, the investigation started, how could I move my whole life to Australia? obtain a sponsorship? a sustainable job? and settle in the land down under?

The first step was to confirm whether my frame of thinking was logical, I mean it was a major life-changing decision, moving away from family, friends. So, after meeting with close friends, family, and even my work colleagues the response let's just say was not that great.

"How will you get your visa?"

"Why move to the other side of the world"

"Impossible, you know how many people want to move to Australia, join the queue"

"Are you crazy, your family is here, why move away from us?"

"It can't be done"

"Why don't you focus your efforts here in the UK?"

So, this made me ponder for a while, why is everyone so against the idea, why not take on the challenge for something new. Then as if by magic my mind clicked, the penny dropped, why? Really it was quite simple, maybe because most people follow a set pattern, if something is too difficult why do it, no one else they know had tried or is embarking on the challenge so why do it?

The Trigger:

I was not going to accept no, or it can't be done as an answer if anything I was more motivated than ever to follow my goal. But how, what steps did I need to take to make this a reality. I would need to think outside the box, do what no one else was doing, it was time for action.

One morning on my usual 30-minute commute to work, crammed against the window of a busy London underground carriage I started thinking.

"How can I follow my dream, what tactics must I follow, what is it I need to do that most of the population would not"

But wait a minute, I work in sales, I sell for a living, why can't I sell myself and influence a company to sponsor me? What can I offer? what is my value add?

My company training, and direct managers embedded into me that you need to take action and pick up the phone, in order to develop your sales pipeline, and get the results needed to hit your sales targets.

So why was I not applying the same concept in my personal life; I needed to act, and fast.

Accepting the Challenge:

So, I got to work, I googled the top 5 competitors for my company in Australia, I obtained the generic, and director emails, then I got to work.

What was the content of the email? What was the approach? Well, the content was rather simple; the goal was to get some sort of interest from a similar company willing to employ and sponsor me overseas.

"Hi, my name is Matthew, and I work with one of your competitors in London, I would be keen to have a chat with you, and perhaps share a few ideas"

"Ultimately, I am looking for a new opportunity in Australia, and sharing my experience/ideas within the Sales, and B2B Marketing space to help drive your business forwards"

"Let me know when you're free to discuss further"

As you can see, the content was rather simple, and straightforward, and out of the 5 companies I emailed, two came back me, one was rather generic "we will see you if you get here" the other and the game changer was an email from the MD of a leading B2B Lead Generation in Sydney who was open to meeting with me and discussing how I could add value to their business.

What Happened Next?

Well it all kind of went uphill from there, one simple email that opened the door to a world of opportunity, within a week I met with the director in London, within 3 weeks the sponsorship visa process had started, and by 6 months I was sitting in my new office in the heart of sunny Sydney.

All because I decided to act, take a chance, and tried an approach that was not unique, but who else would have thought to follow the same approach. Remember this was back in 2008, Linked-In was still quite primitive, and the first iPhone had just come onto the market.

A Happy Ending

Well not quite, coming to Australia, and settling into a new country can be rather stressful, although I was in one of happiest cities in the world. During my 8 years in Australia, I was made redundant, and lost my job twice, managed to get two separate companies to re-sponsor me, and then complete my Australian Citizenship.

"Trust me, losing your job on a sponsored visa is not a pleasant experience, I had the challenge of finding a new company to take on my sponsorship within 30 days or be deported; luckily I had built a strong network of well-connected friends that helped me get through these challenging times"

Within a few years, I met the love of my life, got married bought a house, got some great friends, travelled around some fantastic locations within Australia, and progressed up the corporate ladder.

What did I learn?

What if I never sent that email, what if I never took the initiative to reach out to those 5 competitive companies in Australia. What if I took the advice of my friends and family, and stayed put in the UK, how would things have turned out? – I guess we will never know.

One of the greatest lessons I learned in life was to take my learning experiences in sales and then apply them within my personal life. Of course, you need to make some adjustments to match your own unique life, however, taking action will get you to where you want to be on a personal and professional level.

- Do I apply for that new role within my company? am I ready to take on a new challenge?

- Should I organize my finances? do I have time to implement a plan that will take me to financial freedom?

- Do I invest in property? do I take the risk and invest in my future?

- Will I have the courage to approach that girl I like?, could they be the love of my life?, my soul mate?, well if I don't try I will never know.

- I have always wanted to take flying lessons; is it possible, don't you have to be super intelligent to fly a plane?

Life is a journey, full of wonder and excitement, heartache, pain, and many wonders. You need to follow your dreams, take initiative to take the next step with your career, business, personal life, finances, whatever it may be.

4. The Little-Know Reason Why Cold Calling is Twice as effective in 2019.

We are now in a new age of technology, with lightning fast internet speeds, and cloud-based technology evolving at an alarming rate, tech start-ups are popping up like fast food restaurants.

The world has access to immense amounts of information, we are now able to communicate on a level never seen before in previous years (social media, messaging tools, VOIP, and video collaboration tools); which is truly helping to bring the world closer together, and assist businesses from all continents to work more effectively.

But is it too much?

Since the release of the Apple iPhone in 2007; new applications now allow us to communicate on the move, at home, and in the office. We are now being bombarded with information, marketing, promotional offers from all angles; and at all hours of the day.

Information is great, however, too much of it can start to make people feel very negative against these communication methods.

"Just this morning I opened Linked-in, to find 7 promotional in-mails (all with the same generic pitch), 10 emails from web developers, and SEO specialists, and before we hit mid-day I was cold called by a real estate company, 2 telco providers, and an insurance broker, so even someone like me who is truly passionate about sales and marketing was starting to get a little overloaded, and frustrated, and I do this for a living"

So, What Does This Mean?

Be honest; how much of your time is taken up by having your work PC, Phone or tablet glued to your eyes?

"I remember my first trip to Hong Kong, traveling on the underground system in 2012, there would be a continuous announcement advising people to keep their eyes looking ahead of them, and not locked on phone screens to avoid accidents"

As salespeople we are becoming more reliant on other communication methods, emails, social media, and blogging; which are all great channels to utilize but using them alone is simply not enough; we are becoming lazy, and less personal

So How is this relevant to Cold Calling?

We are busier than ever before, with our attention spans dropping by the day. So how are sales people truly able to get their message across to their target market with emails, or social media if their target audience is so bogged down that checking or replying to an email may be placed at the bottom of the priority list?

Getting someone out of their busy zone is a skill; by picking up the phone and calling your clients or prospects, you are able to pull someone out of their daily schedule and get their full attention, even if only for a brief while.

"During the first few months of running my business I assumed that the 'I am not interested' or 'send me an email, we are looking at this in the future' were just fob offs to get me off the phone. I would have never imagined that 6 months later the same prospect that insisted they were not interested would become one of my highest billing clients"

Just because you get a no on the first call, does not mean you will get a no in the future, you need to nurture your prospects, and I am not just talking about sending mail chimp marketing emails, you need to call them for a chat, and stay on the radar.

Is it becoming harder too Cold Call?

The simple answer is yes; people are busier than ever before; we are working longer hours; improved technology means that we are always switched on to the office; people truly value their personal and family time more than ever before.

Having someone call you and interrupt your already busy schedule is only going to frustrate people further.

"I remember my first job in London 2007 as a Tele-Prospector; I felt like I could call anyone, say anything, nervous or confident; It seemed very easy to reach the right people and get their attention for 5-10 minutes; now in 2017/18 you have to work smarter to reach your audience, and engage in the right way to get their true attention"

The 30-second myth to get your prospects attention on the phone is well and truly dead; you need to be doing this within the first 5-10 seconds; This takes a unique skill set, and solid sales experience.

So Why Cold Call?

Picking up the phone and calling your target audience is still one of the best communication methods to reach people. By taking them out of their busy stressful day (even for a small moment), you can grab them into your world, you are connected, and engaging (now you can start to build a trusted relationship).

Now you have the opportunity to open a solid conversation with your target audience, and remind them of that email or in-mail you sent; you are able to start the relationship building; thus, the sales cycle begins (or ends if you are quickly able to qualify them out).

"When I first started my Tele-Prospecting business in back in 2015, I spent 4-6 hours a day cold calling new prospects; with no clients, or referrals it was critical that the business starting building pipeline to ensure that we had a healthy flow of new opportunities, and cash flow; this has now resulted in a healthy flow of clients, improved cash flow, and room for positive and scalable business growth"

How can I be more Effective on the Phone?

So, in conclusion; with the world becoming busier, and busier every day in the workplace, and within our personal lives, with very limited free time, and an ever-decreasing attention span, it is critical that salespeople adopt new strategies when cold calling their target market.

Business owners, MD's, CEO's, IT Managers, and I guess humans in general, are all looking for the same thing; how can I solve my problems? look good in my career? and get more business through the door? so they can spend more time focusing on the core areas of their business, get more quality time with the family, or focus on that new hobby which has been put off for so long.

Below are some quick tips to help get those brain juices flowing:

- **Get your point across sooner**, make sure you get their attention early on the call.

- **Ask for Permission to sell**, practice a good introduction that excites your target market, and gets them asking questions early in the discussion – Think about client examples and pain points that your service or product helps to resolve.

- **Understand your target market**, is your service, or product going to interest them? What are their potential challenges?

- **Write a good script or guideline document**, practice, rewrite and practice again until it works.

- **Be conscious of your audience's time**, are they busy; acknowledge that they are busy, set up another time to talk.

- **Utilize other channels, such as email, and Linked-In, with your cold calling strategy–** (remind your target audience over the phone of that email you sent – while you have their attention).

- **Be consultative**, don't just go with a set of standard questions, write down the responses, and then ask new questions that are tailored to the responses of your audience.

- **Ask why?** – If your audience is not interested, always ask why? – provide a couple of options why they may not be interested to help ignite the conversation.

- **Get Referrals**, if you are not speaking with the right person, don't let that call go to waste (especially if they are senior (MD, GM) ask them politely for a referral.

- **Send a Calendar Invite** – (If you are struggling to reach your prospect, maybe don't harass them with calls every day; try sending them a calendar invite for 1 week away, the worst that can happen to you is the invite will be declined, or the prospect may suggest another time to catch up.

5. The Invisible Structural Problems Crippling Your Sales Teams Success!

After 3 months of running my own company, I soon realized that being a sole prop involves allotting of hard grafting; and quite simply, you can't switch off, without you the business will not run, projects won't function, and cash flow will diminish.

So, it was time to build a team, and hire my first employee, but how do I find, and train them, will they be successful, and understand my business; so many questions were going around my mind. Either way, it was time to take the leap from a consultant to the business owner.

Building the team to 2, and then 3 seemed quite straightforward, surely, I just replicate the exact same process as the previous sales rep? well yes, if humans were programmed like robots; the reality is very different,

So How to Identify these Problems?

Working for a number of SMEs, and Large Corporations had already given me firsthand experience in identifying key structural setups that could either motivate your team, increase loyalty, and help grow your team or business, or completely destroy your team, resulting in your good people looking elsewhere, and lost the opportunity for growth.

The same problems that occur in large corporations are also present in the medium, and smaller start-up organizations.

"Imagine this, if you run a small company with 4 sales reps, and say you are having performance issues with 2 of them; that is 50% of your staff; now compare the same ratio to a large corporation. That's like 1,000 reps in a large global corporation with 2,000 sales reps going on performance management; these issues can seriously hinder a company from growth opportunities"

So how do we spot issues within our own team or business; I guess we can start by asking key questions that may lead us to the root of the problem.

5.1 Do I have the right people that help my growth strategy?

From all my years in the corporate world, the one thing that has stuck with me with every role, job, challenge, and the project is the attitude. By having the right attitude, you are far more likely to succeed and do well than others who are always looking for the next excuse to why something cannot be done.

"My first job out of University started with a small boutique telemarketing company in London; it was a very successful company, that hired young, hungry, and energetic people, I would like to think I was one of them.

"After pulling my guts out to hit my number, and then win to exceed as one of the top performers of the month for 3 months straight, I could not work out why others would simply try and find excuses to why I was successful"

"Oh, he is faking his results"

"What's the point in trying, he is only going to beat us anyway"

"The job pays so little, he works way too hard"

"We live for the base salary, who cares about commission"

"And so on; as you can imagine the wingers were soon put in line, left the company, or asked to leave"

Get to Know your Team!

So as a manager and people leader take a good look at your employees, are they happy? Do they come up with excuses when you give them a task or project? Is work, and life simple to hard?

Perhaps you could provide some solid training, and coaching to bring them up to speed, or provide some assistance with a personal issue; it could also be a great opportunity to let them see that perhaps the role is just not the right fit for them.

5.2   Am I hiring Reps with an excellent track record, yet they fail in my team?

So, it is time to hire a new member to the team; you find an absolute cracker, who smashed their numbers year after year, mind-blowing references, of course, you hire them; but they don't turn out to be the sales guy you hired, what happened? what did I do wrong?

"After 4 years of working for a large global tech company out of Sydney, I decided it was time for a new challenge, time to venture to greener pastures, so I thought. Interviews were completed, the offer was on the table, so I went for it"

"My first few weeks were very inspiring, training in San Francisco (fantastic), a new laptop, a great team, but that is where it ended; where was my manager, where is the structure to follow; then it hit me like a stone, I needed to work this out myself"

"I lasted a good 6 months in the role; needless to say, it was not for me; and the reality behind the situation, well I was simply not suited for the culture and role. The whole company was set up like an entrepreneurial hub; you made your own decisions, and plans, failed and learned; I was not accustomed to this, coming from a multi-billion dollar tech company with structure, and a clear direction to follow"

Will my New Reps Fail?

So, this one experience taught me, that just because you were an absolute sales gun in your previous role, does not automatically mean that you kill it in the next role. I was not a cultural fit, the support mechanisms I became so accustomed to, had disappeared, and by the time myself and the management team figured it out, well it was too late.

The real challenge in avoiding successful sales reps from failing in your organization is making sure you ask the right questions during the interview process; if the culture is not the same as what they are used to (for example relaxed, laid back vs boiler room, or micromanaging), then it is critical that you a) set this expectation up front with the rep, and b) work on the areas of improvement from the start.

5.3   Do I have high achieving Reps that quit once the team grows?

So, you have some great sales reps, high achievers who are all pushing the business forward in terms of growth, fantastic. You start hiring new staff to take on the new workload, then for some unknown reason your high achievers decide it is time to quit; what happened?

"A few years back at large tech company out of Sydney I witnessed a very similar situation; the business unit was growing, they needed to hire, but after a few months the reps were not happy, motivation was at an all-time low, and people were leaving, but why?"

"Of course, rumors spread, and then there is gossip; however, the underlying factors behind the poor motivation were much clearer, for a start when you hire new reps, they need a territory to manage, and there is only a certain number of companies to prospect across one state or country, so the only solution is to split the territories , but KPI's stayed the same, well they actually nearly doubled"

"This leads to allot more pressure being placed on the team to succeed with a much smaller territory; furthermore, due to the increased KPI's management were starting to come down on even the most experienced reps on performance management; the situation did not look pleasant. The reality was all the experienced reps decided to leave, pay rises were cut, and there was now no real incentives to stay"

So How Do I Avoid Losing my Best Talent?

"If you look after your staff, they'll look after your customers. It's that simple" – Sir Richard Branson,

There really is no one size fits all for this situation; however, one crucial factor to look at before you grow your team is the capacity elements of your business, or division.

Are your reps already overworked managing multiple territories, or are they spending most of the time working on admin, and completing complex excel sheets which takes them away from the core duty of selling.

If the core issue is poor sales tools or too much time spent on non-core sales activities, then hiring more reps may worsen the problem, instead of fixing it, and it may be time to explore the core problems of your structural setup.

However, if it is simply a case of too many territories for one rep to manage, or you do not have the resources to manage multiple clients, then it would certainly be time to hire new staff to help meet this new demand.

<u>Lessons Learned!</u>

There are many lessons to learn when running your own team or business; your employees will make or break your success as a leader, so make sure you spend time analyzing them, to help create a positive culture that attracts the right type of people.

Below are a few tips which have helped me over the years to improve as a people manager and create the right attributes to enable success within a team-based environment.

Holding onto your Best Talent:

- **Communicate with your staff on a regular basis** – (Identify issues quickly and help develop and grow your team members to bring out the best in them).

- **Ask your people how you can manage better** – (brainstorm with the team, identify problems together and work on solutions).

- **Quickly Identify staff who have negative attitudes towards the role** – (If your people are not willing to change, then it may be better to part ways, so you can hire people who will help drive your business forward.

Share your Goals, and Achievements with the Team:

- **Share the company goals, and achievements** (do this with the team on a regular basis – (celebrate together; did one of your reps identify a lead that closed, make sure they stand out).

- **Setup regular weekly meetings (and 1:1's with the team)** – (get the team talking, share ideas, observe <u>EQ</u> (is someone not happy, are they having personal problems)?

Hire at the Right Team to Enable Growth:

- **Is cash flow looking positive enough** – (to hire new staff, remember you need a buffer to help sustain the training element (for sales reps it could take 3-6 months before deals start closing).

- **Are your current reps stressed out, overworked** - (then perhaps you need additional resources to manage the workload)?

- **Identify how you will split sales territories** – (will you be adding new territories, and locations to your marketing strategy? or will you be splitting the existing territories? and how will your current sales reps react to this)?

6. Sales People Never Fail, only Sales Managers Fail Their People!

Throughout my career, I have encountered several management styles, cultures, training programs, and motivational techniques which have all helped to shape my own personal views on sales management.

My time in management is very limited, so in no way am I an expert on the subject, this article is simply a reflection on my own experiences, and how I have adapted my own style over the years.

3 Top Management Mistakes I Experienced during my Sales Career.

It is well known that your manager is the number one reason that justifies you staying or leaving from your current job; of course, money has a huge impact, including job responsibilities, and the company culture.

"During my previous years as a sales rep, I came across a range of managers, all with their own styles, personalities, and unique ways of creating motivation throughout the team. Some of these methods truly helped me to find my inner voice, skill set, and motivation, others simple left me sitting on my seat wondering why the hell I was working there"

Creating a Culture of Fear.

Many books have been written that enforce the use of fear to motivate your team; keeping an element of fear helps keep your team's energy on high levels (really does it?) Perhaps for some people it helps to give them a well-deserved kick up the backside; for others it may completely damage the relationship between the employee, manager, and the company.

"Back when I was working for a large company in Sydney, I will never forget one of the department leaders calling all the sales reps into a training session, only to announce a new performance review process. Without going into too much detail, it went something like 'so if you miss your number, you go on a management review, followed by a PIP, then if you do not improve you are out, it is nothing personal, just business' – You can imagine the level of energy over the next 2 weeks, yes that's right zero"

Creating fear is not necessarily a bad thing if it is done the right way, with the right people who deserve to have that fear set upon them; perhaps non-performers. However, there are many other techniques and approaches that help to actually reinforce the fact that you are dealing with people, not just numbers.

Lack of Empathy.

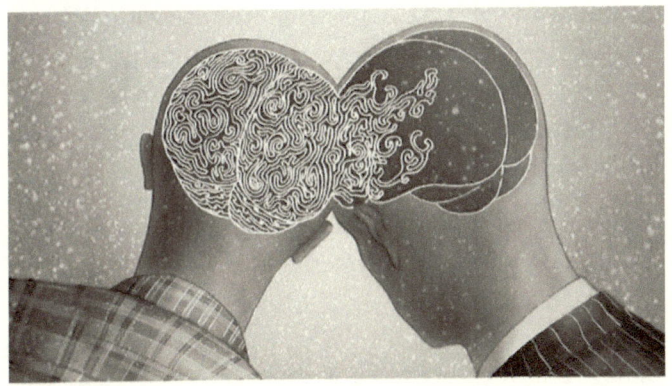

Empathy, the ability to understand and share the feelings of others; this is embedded, and has deep roots in our brains, bodies, and in our evolutionary history. In order to give someone advice, or assistance you have to first understand them; this, in my opinion, is key to being a good manager, who has the ability to sense when an employee is unhappy or upset.

"A few years back I had the opportunity to work in Asia for a large global player; this was a fantastic opportunity to work in one of the most developing countries on the planet. This was my first time working within a completely unfamiliar culture, tropical storms were brewing outside, the streets would be flooded in a matter of moments and getting home would be nearly impossible" So my initial reaction over the first few weeks were to panic, I could not focus on my work, motivation was at an all-time low"

"Now some may say that I should have been the one to approach my direct report to discuss my concerns, however the reality was I just did not feel comfortable enough to do this, instead it sent me down a slippery slope where I ended up leaving the company" – After I left the company, and expressed my reasons for leaving they had no idea that I was upset, scared, and extremely uncomfortable"

People are all unique human beings, not one person can be compared to another, we are all individual in our own ways.

Lacking Effective Sales Tools.

Setting up your sales team with the correct knowledge and tools can be the key to having successful and motivated employees that are also high performers. Sales tools don't have to be physical tools or software, this could be the right guidance, knowledge, or training that helps guide them in the right direction and are tailored to the individual.

"Not long ago I was working for a top tech company out of Sydney as an Account Manager; on Day 1, I was given a laptop, two weeks of training, and a bunch of online learning resources for self-learning and told 'of you go!'. Excitement overload, but this was the first entrepreneurial company I had worked for, and the expectation was you were a self-starter and would hit the ground running from day one; where do I start?"

"When I asked management for guidance, and support, the finger was always pointed back at the training documentation, and online resources 'follow the guides', this did not help point me in the right direction, and most of my time was spent wondering if I was heading in the right direction. It turns out my direction was way off, and without a manager to guide me I ended up at a dead end. – As you can imagine, I did not last very long with this firm; was it the wrong cultural fit for me, possible, or did I just need a bit of guidance and support?"

Having a great set of sales tools, assisted software, and training are all great, but if your sales team don't know how to use them, or effectively implement the tools, then these could be wasted resources. Using the top of range CRM to manage pipeline is all good, but if your sales team lack the basic knowledge of sales management and prioritizing sales opportunities then you will not get the most out of the investment, and you may be left with staff that simply do not understand why they are not using the tool effectively.

Mistakes I Made as a Manager.

So, after years of being managed by others, I finally had the opportunity to experience managing others while working for a large technology company in Australia. A few years later I started my own business, managing a team of highly skilled tele-prospectors across the globe. Little did I know the extent of the challenge I had in front of me, to motivate, manage a team of people with multiple personalities, and motivators, I had to create a strategy and fast.

"If I look back at all my managers over the years, and the amount of grief I gave them, for my own faults, and mistakes I personally made, it makes me wonder. Once you experience management and the challenges it brings, you will never truly be the same person again. I have since called most of my existing managers and apologized for the way I acted, and said thank you for their support over the years; it is not an easy job"

Not Listening.

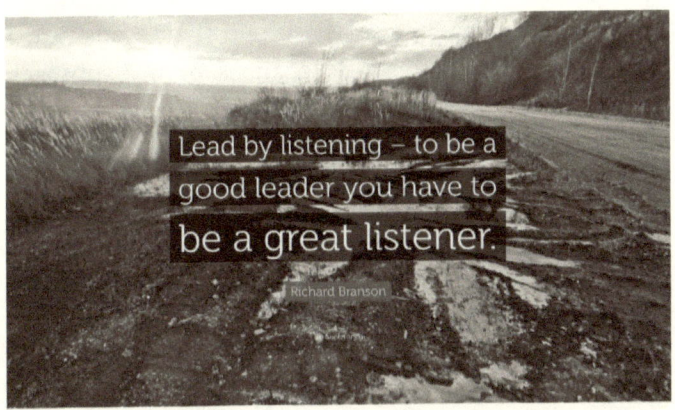

Lead by listening – to be a good leader you have to be a great listener.

Richard Branson

It is well known that salespeople are not all great listeners; (this certainly applies to me) and is a fault that I have been trying to improve for years. Listening is key to understanding people; how can you possibly give good advice if you do not truly understand the other person's pains, challenges, or problems.

"Once again, during my time as a team leader at a large technology company in Sydney, I experienced this hands on. Respect is something that has to be earned and takes time, and at the same time respect and your personal brand can also be destroyed in an instant"

"Every week I would conduct individual weekly catch ups with my team, and each team member would tell me their challenges for the week, and what they needed help with. Before most of my team would tell me the full extent of the issue, I was quick to interrupt with a solution and move on to the next item, without understanding the true story. One day one of my team interrupted me, and said straight out "Are you actually listening to what I say, you keep butting in, and then giving me advice that is not relevant to my situation' I soon realized that they had a point (I was unaware I was doing this), and made changes to my approach straight away, with immediate results.

Being Open to Empathy.

As mentioned earlier in the article, empathy, the ability to understand and share the feelings of others; how can you truly understand someone if you are not on the same wavelengths as they are. Humans experience all kinds of emotions, stress, loss, anger, fear, and so on; as unique people, we all have our own issues (personal or work related), and it is imperative that as a manager you truly understand what people are going through.

"Starting a business has it's challenges, and as an entrepreneur (especially at the start) you are responsible for everything (management, sales, marketing, invoicing, payroll, invoice collecting, training, hiring, and HR) – Put it this way, you learn a lot very quickly, and you make a whole lot of mistakes; it is impossible for you to be good at everything"

"When I first started my marketing agency business, my focus was purely sales driven, get everyone on the phones and drive activity. I would push hard to get the high levels of motivation we needed to be successful, however, I was lacking empathy, some of my team were feeling down, and I simply assumed that this is down to lack of focus. The reality, however, was a series of personal issues that needing addressing, including my management style, listening to what motivates my team, and providing support to help the team move forward with the business"

By providing solid advice, and going beyond the status quo, I found huge loyalty from my staff moving forward

Be a Leader, not just a Title!

One of the key things I have learned in the last 3 years of running my own business is to not just assume that everyone has the same thinking as you. Just because I want the business to be successful and am willing to put in 10-15-hour days, does not mean my team will do the same.

Going back to my previous days working for smaller organizations as a regular employee, I did not really care if the business was making money, I wanted to work, earn my commission then at 6 pm leave and be at home with my family and friends, so why should my staff be any different.

Being a leader means working as a team, gaining a bit of respect, but at the same time having the team work with you, as well as a creating the right culture that works with the people and the business (this can be a massive challenge for both managers and business owners).

"Over the last few years, I have made many mistakes with managing my current team, with so many distractions presence as an entrepreneur it is easy to forget about your team, and just focus on the business goals. As Sir Richard Branson once said, if you look after your staff, they'll look after your customers, it's that simple.

If you look after your staff, they'll look after your customers. It's that simple.

— *Richard Branson* —

"Recently I encountered a situation where I would be asking for help from other business partners in terms of managing my team, and these individuals would talk to my team, and provide advice, discipline actions etc, so I could reinforce the importance of a certain issue such as attendance' – This was not a good move. My team would then question my leadership, am I leading, or simple offsetting the management to someone else? I quickly changed this tactic, and instead would drive all management myself, as a leader this was critical, and once I made the relevant changes I saw an immediate change in my staff who I felt now wanted to work with me out of choice"

<u>You Hired them!</u>

'A Senior Manager ran into his CEO's office to complain about one of his sales reps, who he mentioned was underperforming, and he had enough of them, and wanted them gone. The CEO responds quickly with 'no problem Mark, bring me in the manager who hired him, and I will fire them right now'

At the end of the day as a manager, you are responsible for your staff, if they are not performing, then you need to find a way to help provide the support for them to be successful. And if you hired them, you are even more responsible for their success. If you and the staff agree that the culture is not the right fit, then that is also great, as long as you have done everything in your power to try and make it work.

In Conclusion:

At the end of the day, there is no one solution fits all in terms of management styles, you need to get to know your team, listen to what they have to say. Ask them the simple question, how can I be a better manager, ask what they like, or do not like about your style, and how you can improve.

Create a manage upwards approach with your staff, you can learn a great deal from your team, especially if you are new in the management space.

Once again, I want to reinforce the fact, that I am no expert, I continue to make mistakes every day in the management space, and on occasion offending my team. At the end of the day if we learn from these mistakes, we can all get on-board the same boat, and head to the same destination.

7. Why too many B2B Leads can be just as bad as not enough Leads!

In the early days of running my B2B telemarketing business, it was all-hands-on-deck; every minute was utilized in some way, so we could grow the business, and generate a healthy pipeline for the year, and most critical sign up new clients to drive us forwards.

Never in a million years did I think I would ever be in a position where I could not follow up every call, referral, or web inquiry, it did not seem possible.

"During the first year of business I would spend time writing articles on Cold Calling, and Sales Management; the purpose, to improve our brand, get our name into the market, and utilize another sales channel"

"But then it happened; my first linked an article on cold calling, and campaign management brought in over 50,000 views, that's over 1,000 views a week, with a never-ending the stream of likes, and comments flowing through my linked-in page; but how did this happen?"

As a small business, I simply did not have the resources available to follow up all my leads. Some of the leads were followed up too late and ended up going with a competitor.

Can you really have too many leads?

Honestly, yes 100%, you really can; if you don't have the resources or lead management tools in place to follow up leads in an appropriate time frame, then these leads can be wasted, if they are followed up too late, or not followed up at all.

We are in a new age; businesses are moving faster than ever, new start-ups are appearing every week; a lot of these start-ups are seeing huge growth rates, investors have been found, and within the blink of an eye they are now medium/large sized organizations, with huge market exposure, and interest levels peaking.

The same challenges can also apply to well-established businesses, and even large corporations, who have again seen a massive time of growth, or larger corporations that have not quite found the right lead management process or have an old inefficient setup that delays the lead follow up.

"Back when I working as a sales rep for a large technology company in Australia, we would utilize a number of lead channels (inbound, outbound, email, digital etc.) which would all go through a complex lead assignment process, that required the input of several people. Quite simple the process was just too long, and if key people were away on leave, leads would simple not get assigned or called; this was a great way to waste a good lead; you need to call leads straight away, while there is solid interest"

Implementing Effective Lead Management Processes:

After 17 years of working across multiple sales positions, and industries, I have seen my fair share of lead management tools, and systems. Some companies provide super expensive ERP, CRM, and research tools to help with prospecting, and lead management; however, if the sales reps are not trained correctly to effectively use them, then the tools are wasted. In my case, I simply started using my own processes, and tools that helped progress, and track leads faster.

And in terms of lead management, the most effective processes were the simple ones; cutting out as many approval layers as possible, and having multiple redundancies as a backup, when key people were on leave, or systems went down. By having a simple but effective process, you ensure that all leads are followed up in a suitable time frame.

So what works?

- **Externally Managed –** (Outbound, and inbound channels can be managed by an external company that will qualify leads in real-time then assign the leads when the interest is hot. This process also enables you to qualify out the time wasters, and tire kickers faster; and focus on the genuine leads, which enables sales reps to focus on core revenue driven activities.

- **Separate Lead Generation & Deal Progression –** (Separate the cold calling, and deal progression/closing activities). Either hire your own ISR's, or telemarketers to specialize in cold calling or use an external agency (as mentioned above) to manage this process). This leaves your sales reps free to progress and close new business.

- **Reducing the Approval Layers –** (For medium to larger organizations with multiple sales reps, it makes sense to have a 3rd party person within the company to assign leads to the sales staff. However, this process needs to be super simple; when warm leads are assigned they need to be followed up within 24 hours. For urgent leads, they need to be directed to the reps sooner, via an email or even call (while the interest is warm).

- **Efficient Processes for your Sales Team –** (Sales reps are expensive, so it is critical that you have reps working for you that are closing and driving deals forward) – A huge part of this is reducing unnecessary workload. – Simplify the admin, outsource as much of the process as possible, and have your reps working on a healthy pipeline, and driving qualified leads forwards.

What about Implementation?

"My business recently conducted a number of campaigns for a large tech company out of Sydney that was experiencing issues with lead management. The company was growing at a staggering rate, interest levels were peaking, however with limited resources, it was difficult to follow up every lead from multiple sales channels, they needed help"

"The solution; use our telemarketing services to manage the inbound leads from multiple locations, follow up digital marketing downloads, and conduct cold calls into new industries and run test marketing across multiple markets. Our client now has an efficient lead management strategy in place, which is manageable, and scalable, with our activities creating new business leads, opportunities, and appointments for the entire sales engine across multiple geographic regions"

You need a Scalable Sales team.

As businesses grow there is more demand placed on key areas of the business, new teams are built, departments are formed, and processes are created to make sure the organization runs effectively. Companies which require a big sales presence in the B2B space will need an effective sales team, that scales as it grows.

"Running my own business has given me the opportunity to learn, fail, and create effective practices to help assist with the internal growth. As the sole director, I am responsible for running the whole show, including recruitment, training, sales, invoicing, collecting, marketing, and so much more. So, it was a quick learning curve to make sure that as my client base grew, the sales team also grew effectively, and scaled in line with the requirements of the business"

"Having an effective lead management program takes time, creating recruitment, interview, and training processes also take time, however, once they are set in place and the right systems and tools are implemented the scalability issues become much easier to tackle" – (And this certainly does not happen overnight).

For effective lead management, you need a process that works for your business; if you are growing fast and are simply short on resources to follow up leads, then you can look at hiring a team of ISR's to carry out your lead qualification. Alternatively, you could also outsource this service to another organization; with both options enabling your sales reps to focus on their core role; deal progression, and revenue generation.

Having the right sales mix?

Every company is different, so this really depends on your type of B2B business, and perhaps the setup you believe would worst best for your organization; a lot of this will come with trial and error.

- **Develop your Lead Management Internally: -** You may decide to keep everything in-house, having a team of ISR's and perhaps telemarketers managing your inbound, and outbound lead channels, then filtering qualified leads to the relevant sales reps.

- **Outsource: -** Another option is to outsource the whole lead management (inbound, and outbound, including digital marketing) to another organization that specialize in this field. This will reduce the resources, and management constraint of your staff, and will enable you to provide your sales reps with a healthy supply of qualified leads, with the non-qualified leads left with the external company to manage, until they are ready to be delivered as a solid opportunity to your business.

- **Combination of Outsourcing, and In-house Strategies:** Combining both internal and outsourced lead management can also be a great strategy to help with the strong growth of your B2B sales engine. Having the internal ISR's and telemarketers focus on the core products, with the outsourced agency managing perhaps the digital inbound inquiries, or spill over such as event management.

In Conclusion:

As covered above, there are many strategies that you can implement to help you manage your B2B Sales Pipeline, especially during times of heavy growth. It is imperative that companies follow up new leads in a timely matter; with the speed of business in this day and age the difference of 1-2 days can make the difference to a 'yes we are interested 'to 'sorry your competitor called us first'.

Outsourcing your Lead Management via telemarketing channels is a great way to take the strain off your company resources and focus your time on other core aspects of the business.

8. Selling is Believing! - Why You Can Only Sell What You Believe in!

I was young, inexperienced, and making a tonne of money; after my first month the pay cheque arrived, a whopping 7,000 pounds, this is awesome I thought, 'I can really make this much money'. I felt like a Rockstar, I shouted drinks every Friday and bought expensive toys, I honestly felt invincible.

And then, one day I saw a customer service rep crying in the lunch room, the reason shocked me; I had no idea that customers were rarely getting past their first project. I heard a bunch of rumours that the company was terrible and run poorly, I even called an ex-client by accident and they started yelling at me.

Then I decided to dig a bit deeper, and quickly discovered the truth, it crushed me, I could not believe our clients thought this way about our services. Furthermore, with growing customer complaints, and the constant push to sell a solution that did not in practice perform the way it was supposed to, it really started to damage the team morale and motivation across the company.

After a few months, I simply stopped believing in what I was selling, the model was not working the way I was told it would. The constant negativity played hard on my mind and health, and this slowly started to show through everything I did; call levels dropped, my attitude turned sour, and most critically my heart was just not in it anymore.

Furthermore, sales reps starting quitting, I struggled to get repeat business, and the company very quickly lost its best people, leaving them with a few robots that simply did what they were told to do.

Do you even believe in what you are selling?

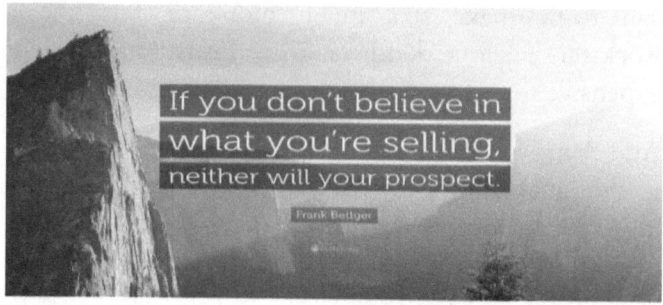

If you don't believe in what you're selling, neither will your prospect.

Frank Bettger

You start working for a great company, get settled into the role, but quickly realize that the solution or product you are selling is playing in the wrong market, is not suitable for the target audience, or simply does not do what it is supposed to.

I was simple, too young, too junior and too focused on making short-term money, with minimal empathy for clients, and no care for repeat business or referrals for the organization I was working for. Without any consideration for my future reputation, or personal brand, soon my mind, and body were feeling very bad; despite the high pay.

A few years after I left the organization, the company started to struggle, and soon after they shut down, and were acquired and rebuilt from the ground up from a competing firm.

<u>Only Sell what you truly believe in!</u>

After working my way through several sales roles, and product offerings, I soon came to the realization that to be successful long-term, progress through your career, or excel in your business, you truly need to believe, and care in what you do for a living.

Whether you are selling second-hand cars, or multi-million dollar tech solutions, without this, you will damage not just your reputation, but also your mind, and soul for future selling activities.

"I remember the countless training sessions in previous companies where half the sales team would fall asleep after the first 20 minutes; motivation and sales were down, everyone knew that the solution was very challenging to sell, and did not meet the expectations of the client, but we continued pushing, and grinding away until the lights burnout"

Reaching Ongoing Success:

It took a long time for me to change my perception of sales, selling just for the sake of selling, and making commission was never a long-term goal, I needed a think long term, and it had to start sooner rather than later.

So, a few years later I took on the challenge of setting up my own agency, with this mindset ready, could it really be that easy? Would I fall back on old habits?

"I remember very clearly, my first year in business, excitement raging, it was a high that I could not explain to anyone. But with this came massive amounts of stress, there was no more monthly salary, my expenses were increasing, I needed to make money fast"

As a result, I quickly started tailoring solutions that were outside my original offerings and were not part of my business, but they met the client's interest. Once again, I was back at my old habits, simply getting cash in the door and not really helping my clients succeed.

One of my first few clients, a great guy who spent a shed load of money on setting up his business and needed help with new business development. I was excited, but his expectations were high, he mentioned to me several times that he truly relied on me to get business, or he was in trouble. Of course, I said yes, let's do this without realizing the long-term focus. Yes, we did a great job for them, but our goals were very misaligned, and he ended up shutting down his business due to a lack of sales.

Looking back, I certainly made a few mistakes in the early days, working with clients that did not see the value in the offerings I was providing the market, and simple bowing down and changing everything to what they wanted. The result, once again I felt bad about selling something I did not truly believe in, working with the wrong type of client, which ultimately ended in a damaged brand.

So, what happened when I changed?

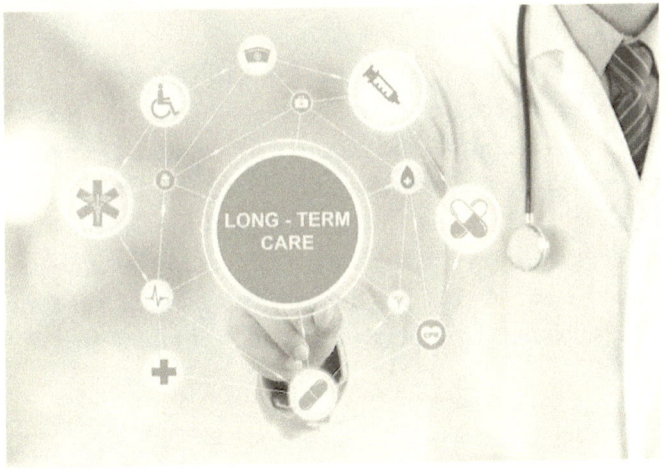

After a few months of settling into the business and working on the true value of my proposition (what I truly believed worked), I soon started turning away prospects and clients, or referring them to my competitors, that I could not help long term or be not aligned in the right way to benefit from what I had to offer. In my experience, this is one of the hardest things you can do, but people will respect you for it, and you will start to attract the type of clients that you want and build long-lasting relationships with them.

"I remember very clearly the first client I turned away; we had a proposed project for 3 months on the table, worth over $23,000; he wanted a 30% price reduction, I was tempted and on the call I remember putting my hand over mouth so I could muffle out the 'yes let's do it'; instead I stuck to my guns, kept my pricing as it was, and expressed the value once again. I ran straight to the bathroom and vomited; I just turned down one of my biggest deals, what was I thinking; I hadn't even taken a salary in 10 months.

At the start I made less, then I could have done in the short term because I planned to be here for the long haul. I saw competitors come and go, and after time soon realized the red flags to look out for. Only after I stuck to selling what I believed in, did I reach ongoing success, and this is exactly what I build my business on today; I am in this for the long run, and I want my own sales reps to believe in the quality of what they are selling.

9. The Secret Recipe to Avoid Ghosting that No One Talks About.

The following article may be of interest to sales leaders, and business owners who would like to understand why sales prospects go quiet or have experienced ghosting during the sales process and would like to explore the best practises to follow to get the most effective results.

Why are you ghosting me?

My first sales job after University 16 years ago was a big eye-opener. Learning the basics of sales prospecting, pipeline management, relationship building, and deal progression, set me up for success for the rest of my professional career.

During my first month, I cold-called and qualified a red-hot prospect; it was all going so well – there was a compelling need, the decision maker was present, and solid value was brought to the table.

Agreements were made to touch base again in 2 weeks to discuss and run through the proposal and discuss time frames to start the project. It was a sure thing!

Well, at least that's what I thought.

Let the ghosting commence:

Two weeks passed, and no response. Another two weeks, and still no response; what was happening?

Did I do something wrong during the sales cycle that caused offence, or did I fail to demonstrate the right value the prospect was expecting? I was at a loss.

Then the desperation sets in!

Should I research the prospect more, perhaps? Maybe I can find something on the industry that would prove useful for the company?

Then, the response.

"Currently investigating, will get back to you soon."

I started asking myself, so what does that mean? At least it's a response.

So, we are back on track?

Well, that's what I thought. But again, two weeks passed, then three, and still no response.

But then, a final response.

"We will not be moving ahead with your proposal but thank you for your time."

That's it. So, what did I do wrong, why did they not move forward? In my case, I was lucky to get some solid and constructive feedback.

The Real Reason for Ghosting

Three weeks after touch point, I decided to throw a quick call in and see if I could get to the bottom of the lost opportunity.

The real reason shocked me!

The whole time, my prospect was interested but was insanely busy, and they decided not to move forward with our proposition <u>due to the constant follow-ups.</u>

So, what is Ghosting?

According to the Oxford Dictionary, Ghosting is defined as *'the practice of ending a personal relationship with someone by suddenly and without explanation withdrawing from all communication.'*

At the end of the day, B2B Sales revolves around humans, which means ghosting is a real possibility as humans by nature are very unpredictable.

It's easy to sabotage yourself!

In my case, I was moving too fast for the prospect and quite simply, I scared them away.

So why did I do this? – I was afraid of moving too slow. What if they talk to a competitor? They might think I am not interested in them anymore, and so on. – Perhaps the fear of loss?

When I went back through my follow up attempts, emails, and calls, it made a lot more sense. I was following up way too much with the prospect.

So how do we avoid ghosting?

Ultimately, there's no one solution that answers the ghosting phenomenon. The more seasoned and experienced you are as a sales professional, the easier it is to avoid.

Over the years, I have learned to better qualify opportunities, and spent more time in the discovery stages, to make sure I add true value before ever talking about the value proposition.

Top Tips

Below are some useful tips to help you avoid falling into the ghosting trap:

1. **Qualify, qualify, qualify** – Did the prospect simply ask you for pricing? Or did they seem uninterested on the call, and simply asked for a proposal to get you off the phone?

Ask more discovery questions.

Research the company and its industry, get news insights, read LinkedIn posts, personalise your approach.

Avoid talking about your solutions, benefits, etc. Rather, make it about them!

2.   **Set time frame expectations**. – Did you force the next follow up appointment onto your prospects, or did you genuinely ask them when they think would be the best time to follow up?

Put it back onto your prospect. Ask when they would like to be followed up next.

Agree to a mutual time and date, and even set a meeting invite as a reminder to make sure there is a solid expectation.

3.   **Do NOT act desperate** – Yes, I know it sounds obvious, right? But when you are failing to hit your sales quota and your salary or commission is paying the mortgage, all humans will act like humans; as a business owner, it can get even worse.

Control your emotions. If all you are thinking about is calling a prospect to get a contract signed, then change your activity. Go for a walk, hit the gym, or do some prospecting.

Improve your pipeline, make more calls and attend more sales meetings, the more deals on the table the less desperate you will become.

4.   **Act like a professional** – Use the right language, speak like a CEO, spend time understanding their business, have confidence, and ultimately be the subject matter expert in everything you do.

Record your own voice. Are you sounding desperate, nervous, or angry with your tonality? If so, you need to change this.

Try different questions and have the right consultative approach that deep dives into your prospect's business pains.

Listen, listen, and listen some more. – Ever heard the saying "two ears, one mouth"? Well, most salespeople are bad listeners (including myself). Bite your tongue, take notes, and do not interrupt.

5.   **Qualify out** – Sometimes the best answer or response you can hear in sales is a solid "No." Great, now it's time to focus on other prospects who are interested.

Thank the prospect for their time and send a quick email apologizing for whatever you may have done to make them disengage from the sales process.

Simply close them out of your CRM, delete them, or set a task 3-months into the future for a follow-up call. Out of sight, out of mind.

10. Why NO B2B Sales are made on Social Media!

You arrive at your desk on Monday morning, settle into your usual routine, and perhaps start sipping on a latte, or cappuccino. You scan through your emails and respond as appropriate, then you flick over to LinkedIn and InMail account, dreading the spam emails that await your opening.

"Hi, this is Mike from XYZ IT support. I noticed we had a LinkedIn connection in common and thought we should connect."

"Do you need IT managed services? We offer Low-cost blah blah blah"

Some do grab my attention but are quickly forgotten as I switch back over to my daily routine, proposals, sales calls, and general operational duties.

Occasionally, I remember the odd InMail that stands out, especially if they are creatively written, and sometimes I will even respond if I have time.

But one question always hangs over me: why does no one call me? My phone and mobile are both on my profile and company website.

Have we forgotten the art of using the phone?

It's a Social Media Tsunami!

Run for your life! Talk about information overload; we are exposed to so much online advertising, B2B, and B2C selling pushed on multiple platforms including <u>Facebook</u> and <u>LinkedIn.</u>

You only must look online to purchase a new item, and next thing you know you are being bombarded by promotional items from multiple vendors offering a range of bells and whistles.

And to top it all off, when it comes to communicating with people, you must choose between a multitude of communication channels including WeChat, WhatsApp, Viber We Chat, Messenger, Skype, and InMail.

I have seen a prospect flat out refuse to deal with a real estate agent in Asia because the agent did not use an iPhone and could not communicate on their preferred iMessage platform.

So, have we forgotten the basics? What happened to using the good old-fashioned phone, or simply sending an SMS?

Is selling becoming harder?

There is a ton of literature, articles, and information that pushes the argument that selling is simply becoming too hard. Is this really the case, or are we simply not trying hard enough and becoming smarter in our approach?

"Sitting at my desk only one year into the business, I was on my 30th call of the day, and received my 30th we are not interested, or 'sorry, it's all driven internally', or 'no budget, or we are using someone else"

What was I doing wrong? I mean, come on, 50 calls a day for 3-4 hours a day — isn't that enough? Surely someone must bite; I thought to myself, *"What the hell am I doing wrong?"*

According to Harvard Business Review, <u>63% of sales people are now failing to meet or exceed quota</u>, with <u>55.8% of sales people meeting or exceeding it</u>. So whatever way you look at it, half of all B2B salespeople are simply not making the grade.

We are selling at the age of the empowered buyer who has access to more information than ever before — significantly delaying the buying process.

According to Gartner, 88% of surveyed customers reported that information they encountered during the purchase decision was high quality, but this also overwhelmed them. Gartner also states that 44% of customers worry that they've missed a better option every time a purchase is made.

So, sell better?

Is it really that simple? We just sell better!

Yesterday I watched Arnold Schwarzenegger's motivational video titled *"The Video That Broke the Internet"* where Arnold gave some insights on his success, challenges, and how he overcame problems in his life that ultimately made him successful.

During the video he mentioned how you should sleep early and get a good 6-hours sleep, then someone from the audience shouts *"What 6! You mean 8, right?"*

Arnold responds with *"What, you think 6 is not enough? Sleep Faster!"*

Brilliant, right?

So yes, it really can be that simple. Become a sponge for knowledge, research your target markets, read up on their industries, news, trends, and become a subject area expert.

So how can I get better at selling?

So, you want to get better at selling, smash your quota, and make a ton of money? Well, start reading, researching, picking up the phone, talking to your network, cold calling, and using technology to help make your selling more efficient. Draw up a plan!

Here are a few tips to get you started:

1) **Use Social Media** – Yes, research your prospects, post articles, respond to your network's posts, share other posts, build a brand, and get noticed.

2) **Pick Up the Phone** – Call new prospects every day, research them on Google and LinkedIn, read up on their industries, and come up with a killer pitch using this new intel.

3) **SMS** – People still message each other via text messaging. Start using this tried and tested tech which is not being over utilized with spam. It really works, try it.

4) **Combo Prospecting** – Combine your selling techniques phone, message, SMS, LinkedIn InMail, and email. Then see what happens. Does it seem like communication overload? Try it and let me know! – Also read "Combo Prospecting" by Tony Hughes who completely nailed this approach in his book.

5) **Stop Selling** – Here's the thing, people are really sick of taking a call where the first thing that comes out the seller's mouth is *"Would you be interested…"* or *"Have you considered your own death, Mr. Smith?"*

Be a consultant and start with something insightful and relevant to the person you are talking to. Just check their LinkedIn activity!

In Conclusion:

So, are no B2B sales made on social media? Maybe some, but the reality is, they are made by combining all of these channels together (social, phone, email, SMS, and so on).

Make sure you combine your sales approaches, become a sponge for knowledge, and just stop selling, <u>really stop selling and start helping people</u>!

11. Client Testimonies

Committed to bringing Passion and Customer Focus to the Business of Enterprise Applications

"Matt and his team have played a huge part in driving our event audience acquisition programs. Our team have been very happy with the results to date. The MCP team provide great attention to detail and provide the extra care factor when working on our programs. I would highly recommend Matt and his team for similar projects"

Helping Businesses to Fight Cybercrime and Reduce Security Risk.

"My company reached out to MCP for help with their lead management engine. Internally we had a big challenge with many uncalled SQL, and MQL leads –

languishing in the CRM database and desperately needed qualifying. MCP helped solve this challenge by conducting a strategic clean up exercise which involved his team calling and qualifying over 400 leads to help identify new opportunities for the sales team, as well as qualifying out the people with no interest, or not a fit for our company. The team are just excellent, super professional, high attention to detail, and it really felt like they were an extension of our sales team. Would 100% highly recommend MCP for anyone looking for similar projects"

Marketing Leading Storage Solutions

"We engaged Matt Cowan Prospecting to support our team with our BDR/SDR activities across ANZ. From the outset, the team proved their worth with results in the first week. We have enjoyed working with MCP, his team are super professional, and we are very happy with the results. Throughout the entire process we truly felt MCP were an extension of our sales team. My company is currently speaking to MCP regarding other projects across Asia. If you are looking for a trusted agency to manage your BDR/SDR and lead generation activities, then MCP would be a great choice"

Unmatched Data Management and Protection

"We engaged MCP to support Storage Craft's sales enablement activities across ANZ. The MCP team were able to generate results within the first week and this success continued to ramp-up over the quarter. I have really enjoyed working with MCP, Matthew's team are super professional, and we are very happy with the results. MCP has acted as a true extension of our sales team. Storage Craft are currently speaking to MCP regarding other projects across ANZ for 2020. If you are looking for a trusted agency to manage your sales enablement and lead generation activities, then MCP would be a great choice"

The investigation, Cybersecurity, and Information Governance Specialists

"Matt's team are professional and responsive, which I really appreciated as a customer who needed a business partner that understood our needs. The team assisted our organization by setting up the lead generation program swiftly and efficiently and provided qualified leads in a short period for our Sales & Marketing Team. We are currently looking at a second project with Matt, and are happy with the partnership"

Global Leader in designing, building, and servicing critical infrastructure

"Matt's team helped our organization to cleanse call data, including qualifying in the solid opportunities and also removing the unwanted rubbish. This was a critical component to our Sales & Marketing Strategy, and we are very happy with the results that the team achieved. We are looking forward to doing further data cleansing activities in 2019"

The World's first business planning cloud

"I have had the pleasure of working with Matt and his team for nearly a year now, and we have had great results. Matt's team are extremely professional and detailed and we truly value the open communication and added care factor. If you are looking for a trusted telemarketing provider that delivers results, I would definitely recommend Cowan Prospecting!"

Global Specialist in Managing Business Travel.

"Matt's drive, and enthusiasm in making 'Matt Cowan Prospecting' a quality player in the BPO / Outsource industry in a short time is a testament to the hard work, and work ethics of his team. The team helped assist our sales and marketing activities by providing critical data profiling components. If you are looking to outsource, then Matt is definitely a man you should be talking to"

ERP business management software.

"I have had the pleasure of working with Matt and his team for several months now. The team have great skills within the B2B Lead Generation space and are both professional and concise. We are currently on our 2nd campaign, and couldn't be happier with the results. I would highly recommend Matt Cowan Prospecting to other companies looking for professional B2B Tele-Prospecting services"

www.ingramcontent.com/pod-product-compliance
Lightning Source LLC
Chambersburg PA
CBHW020551220526
45463CB00006B/2259